The Changing Japanese Woman

From Yamatonadeshiko to YamatonadeGucci

大和なでしこから大和なでグッチ

日本女性の変化

大和なでしこ
から
大和なでグッチ

The Changing Japanese Woman:

From Yamatonadeshiko to YamatonadeGucci

日本女性の変化

Author Contact· Everott Ofori
Takarazuka University of Art and Design
Tokyo Campus Building 1F-123MBE
7-11-1 Nishi Shinjuku
Shinjuku-ku
Tokyo, Japan 160-0023

http://www.writingexpertonline.com
Email: everettofori@yahoo.com

Typesetting: Everett Ofori
Illustrations: Ahn Soo Kyoung

National Library of Canada Cataloguing in Publication
Ofori, Everett, ····
    The changing Japanese woman : from
Yamatonadeshiko to YamatonadeGucci / Everett Ofori.
ISBN 1-894221-04-4
    1. Women·-Japan. I. Title.
HQ1762.O36 2004 305.42'0952 C2004-900198-1

Acknowledgments

Thanks very much to Mr. Kunihiko Koyama, president of the Edogawa International Friendship Association, Tokyo, Japan, for assistance on this manuscript.

For the short time I have been in Japan it would be presumptuous of me to assume that I have more than a cursory understanding of Japanese society. The willingness of Mr. Koyama and other Japanese to share with me knowledge of their society has been invaluable in giving me the courage to publish this book.

In January, 2003, when I took the first tentative steps towards learning the Japanese language it seemed as though I was embarking on a fanciful project. The superb learning atmosphere at the Academy of Language Arts, Iidabashi, Tokyo, Japan, where I spent a few hours every day not only furnished me with the building blocks necessary for the acquisition of the Japanese language but also provided a window into many aspects of Japanese life.

The learning is by no means over. But being able to write a book in Japanese is enough for me to thank Mr. Wachio Ohinata, Director of the Academy of Language Arts, and his team of dedicated staff who were patient at every turn, encouraging students where necessary but always guiding students with a sure hand towards proficiency in the Japanese language.

It would be impossible in this limited space to list all those who have contributed to what little understanding I have of Japanese society but it will be remiss of me not to try to acknowledge some of these fine individuals.

In addition, I am grateful to Ms. Mutsumi Matsugu, Ms. Naoko Saito, and Mr. Tono Satoshi for reviewing earlier drafts of this manuscript and sharing with me their views on the subject.

Dr. Tian-Bo Deng (Toho University, Chiba) and his wife, Takako, helped to ease my anxieties in my first few months in Japan. Many thanks also to Shinichiro Kumada who provided a comforting voice from time to time.

Thanks also to Mr. Andrew Rouse, Mr. Marcos Takaoka Viera, Ms. Merika Gono, Mr. Emory Georges, Ms. Ooshima, formerly of Appleland Preschool, Tokyo, Ms. Satchiko Nakamura, Ms. Yuka Shiizaki of Kids' Corner, Tokyo, Tomo and Mika Abe, and the Tanaka family of Sen Inn (Funabori) fame.

Introduction by Miki Tomoko

One spring afternoon, about a year ago, Mr. Everett Ofori came to our office for the first time. He asked to have a business card printed for himself. Mr. Ofori had only just arrived in Japan then and was studying Japanese very diligently. Studying Japanese and making a business card - he was indeed at the starting line of the process of finding his place to stand in Japanese society. It makes us happy to think that we were able to help him get started, in however small a way.

大和なでしこ
から
大和なでグッチ
The Changing Japanese Woman
日本女性の変化

Everett Ofori

Later, Mr. Ofori asked us to design the cover of one of the books that he was planning to publish. He showed us the ideas for these books and among them was a book in which he interviewed many Japanese women. He wanted the cover to convey an image of Japanese women. I remember wondering, what IS the image of Japanese women? Being a "Japanese woman" myself, I thought the concept was too vague. How, then, do we appear in the eyes of foreigners? It is surprising how little we know how we ourselves are seen from the 'outside.'

A year went by. Mr. Ofori appeared once again, this time with the manuscript of a book with a curious title. It was this book. I was honestly surprised to hear that he had done the Japanese translation himself. His Japanese is simple, and the book gives an impression that it is a fable. And yet it is a solid "Theory on Modern Japanese Women" with a vivid perspective and realistic touch. This diamond, which Mr. Ofori has cautiously extracted with his delicate sensibilities from his own, first-hand experiences of living in Japan, shines with noble certainty. It makes me ponder how we "modern Japanese women," and myself, will feel about this praise.

Mr. Ofori is very positive, enthusiastic, diligent and hard-working. He has a presence that relaxes people around him and eases our English speech phobia. I am sure there are many Japanese who will help him wherever possible throughout his life in Japan. It is probably his desire to understand, to be understood, and to share his understanding, that will move people to do so. I look forward to subsequent books by Mr. Ofori, wondering what vivid portrait of the Japanese and their world he will paint next.

- Feb 2004 Miki Tomoko

Introduction by Miki Tomoko

　1年前のある春の午後、エバレット・オフォリ氏が私たちの会社に
やってきました。名刺を作りたいということでした。その頃オフォリ
氏は日本で暮らし始めたばかりで、日本語の猛勉強中だったよう
です。日本語、そして名刺。日本の社会で自分の 立つ場所を獲
得するための、スタートラインに彼はいました。ささやかだけれど
私たちも、オフォリ氏のスタートのお手伝いができたのだと思うと、
少し嬉しいのです。

　その次にオフォリ氏は、出版を計画中の彼の何冊かの著書の、
表紙のデザインを考えてほしいといって、アイデアを携えてやって
きました。その中に、国際的に活躍する日本人の女性たちにイン
タビューした著書がありました。「日本女性」をイメージしたデザイ
ン、という話になったのですが、そう言われるとあらためて「？」とな
ってしまったのを覚えています。「日本女性」自身にとって、「日本
女性」のイメージというのは漠然としすぎているからです。ならば、
外国人にはどう見えるのだろう？

　私たちは、自分が「外」からどんなイメージで捉えられているか、
ということを案 外知らないものです。

　あれから1年たって、オフォリ氏はこんどは、ちょっとふしぎな題
名の本の原稿を持って現れました。それが、この本です。彼自身
が日本語訳をしたためたと聞いて、正直、驚きました。読んでみる
と、シンプルな日本語で、やさしい寓話のような印象を受けます。
それでいて、切り口の鮮やかな、リアルな手触りのある「現代日本
女性論」が展開されています。オフォリ氏が体当たりの日本体験
の中から注意深く繊細な感性で抽出したダイヤモンドは、堅く高
貴な確信を帯びていますが、はたして「現代日本女性」たちは、こ
の賛辞をどう受け止めるだろう・・・自身に立ち返って考えさせられ
るところです。

　オフォリ氏は、とても前向きで、熱心で、努力家で、働き者で、英
語対面恐怖症を緩和してくれる、人をくつろがせる雰囲気を持っ

た人です。彼の日本体験の過程で、多くの日本人が手助けできることがあればしようと思うでしょう。オフォリ氏の、理解したい、理解してほしい、理解しあいたい、という気持ちが、たぶん、人を動かすのだと思います。そんなコミュニケーションの中から、こんどはどんな鮮やかな日本人とその世界を描いて見せてくれるのか、次作を期待しながら。

2004. 2　　三木　朋子

The Changing Japanese Woman:

From Yamatonadeshiko to YamatonadeGucci

西洋で、最も人気がある　日本についての
"本"は　何十年も前に,書かれました。
そのために、その"本"の日本についての
考えは少しふるいです。

In the West, some of the more popular books about Japan
were written several decades ago. Not surprisingly, ideas
presented about Japan in these books are a little dated.

でも西洋でその古い考えは、まだつづいています。

Even so, some of these old ideas prevail.

特に、日本人の女性についての考えには、たくさん間違いがあります。たとえば日本人の女性は、"弱い"、とよく言われます。多くの西洋人はまだ日本人の女性を、"大和なでしこ" だと思っています。

In particular, concerning Japanese women, there is no shortage of wrong impressions, for example, that Japanese women are weak. And not a few Westerners continue to think of Japanese women as being Yamato nadeshiko.

"大和なでしこ"ってなに？と、もし日本人のおじいさんに誰かが聞いたとしたら、おじいさんは必ずほほえみます。どうしてでしょう？それは、おじいさんたちは、
"大和なでしこ"について実は話したいからです。

Yamato nadeshiko? What is that?
Well, there is no swifter way to get an elderly Japanese man to smile than to ask him about Yamato nadeshiko. Why? This is because elderly Japanese men relish the opportunity to chat about Yamato nadeshiko.

おおくの日本人のおじいさんは "大和なでしこ" は
日本女性の本当の、すがただと思っています。 "大
和なでしこ" は完璧な女性です。ほかの言葉でいえ
ば日本女性の理想です。

大和なでしこ...

Many elderly Japanese men believe that Yamato
nadeshiko represents what a Japanese woman
ought to be. In other words, Yamato nadeshiko is
the ideal image of a Japanese woman who is true
to her roots.

昔は日本は“大和”と呼ばれていました。そして“なでしこ”は日本にある美しい植物の名前です。その植物はまがりやすいですが、折れにくいです。同じように、日本人の女性達は、柔軟で強いとかんがえられています。本当の“大和”なでしこは、知恵があります。主人には“いいえ”
と言いません。本当の“大和なでしこ”は、主人の為に、犠牲になります。“大和なでしこ”は、主人が出世すると、奥さんも同じように輝くようになります。
“大和なでしこ”は、きれいだし、あたまがいいし、日本の文化や、歴史にも関心があります。

In ancient times, Japan was known as Yamato, and nadeshiko is the name of a beautiful plant in Japan that bends easily but is very difficult to break. In the same way, the Japanese woman was expected to be both flexible and strong. A true Yamato nadeshiko was expected to be wise; she would never say "No" to her husband.

In fact, a true Yamato nadeshiko thinks nothing of sacrificing for her husband and putting him first in every way. After all, the more he succeeds, the more she herself glows.

Yamato nadeshiko is beautiful, clever, and has a great deal of interest in Japanese culture.

でも、そんな素敵な女性達を、今でも見つけること
ができますか？今日の女性達は、もう"大和なでし
こ"？なんて存在しないと思っています。"大和な
でしこ"なんて古いのです。

But in Japan today, is it really possible to find such
a "wonderful" woman as Yamato nadeshiko? Some
say there are only a few left. Others say Yamato
nadeshiko no longer exists and that it's a bit of an
old notion.

今日の女性達は、"大和なでしこ"と言うと、かならふしぎな顔をします。でも、女性達の理解はおじいさんとはちがっています。お爺さんの考える"大和なでしこ"は残念ながらもういません。今日の女性達は"YAMATONADE GUCCI"です。

When modern Japanese women hear the term Yamato nadeshiko, invariably are amused. But the meaning of their laughter differs from that of the elderly Japanese man for whom Yamato nadeshiko is a dream woman. In any case, some Japanese men have given up on the idea of finding Yamato nadeshiko. They say, with a touch of sadness, that today's Japanese women are not Yamato nadeshiko; they are Yamato nadeGucci.

主人を支えるかわりに，GUCCIの時計とか、PRADAの
かばんとかLOUIS VUITTONの財布とか、FERRAGAMO
の靴のことばかり考えています。

Instead of supporting their husbands they think
only about buying GUCCI watches and Louis
Vuitton purses, Ferragamo shoes, and other brand
name goods.

だから今日の女性達は、わがままに見えます。でも、実は，わがままではありません。自由にふる舞っているのです。財布には、お金があるから男性を必要としていません。

As such, Japanese women today come across as being selfish. In truth, it would be unfair to call them selfish. They are just enjoying their sense of freedom, and with wads of yen in their wallets they have no need for a man, do they?

お母さんの生活はつまらなかったです。そのため、今日の女性達はもっと楽しい生活をしようと思っています：海外旅行とか、マツサージとか、エステなど、もっと自由な活動をたのしんでいます。

Today's Japanese woman thinks of the boring, uneventful lives led by her mother and grandmother and is determined to live a more interesting life, one that involves frequent overseas travel, a good massage after a hard day's work, and all the pedicure, manicure, and facials money can buy.

今日の、女性達は、繊細に見えますが、間違えては
いけません。心は強いのです。　実はGUCCIのとけい
や、PRADAのベルトを買うばかりではありません。
日本では、英会話レッスンや、会計士になるための
講習、コンピュータープログラミングのトレーニン
グのようなクラスでも多分男性より女性のほうがた
くさん勉強しています。。

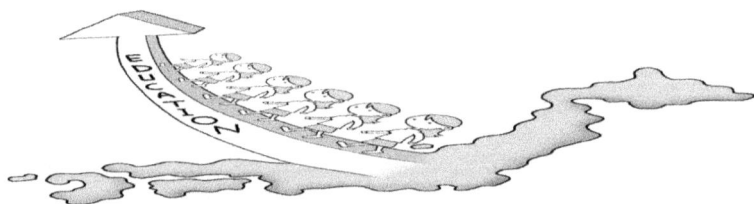

Today's Japanese woman may look soft but make no mistake. She has an iron will, and buying GUCCI watches and PRADA belts are not her only preoccupation. In Japan, step into any learning institution – whether for English language lessons, Certified Professional Accountants (CPA) examination preparation, or computer programming training – and you would probably find more women than men hell-bent on advancing themselves through the acquisition of knowledge.

男性支配の社会は、徐々に変化しつつあります、政治にも、教育にも、ビジネスにも、おおくの女性指導者がでてくるとおもいます。彼女達のお母さんやおばあさんのように家庭に閉じこもっているのではなく、より多くの活動に参加するようになりました。

In Japan, the idea of living in a "man's world" is gradually becoming a thing of the past. Whether in the field of politics, education, or business, a new Japanese woman is emerging – one who can be counted on to participate much more actively than her mother or grandmother, whose domains were largely in the domestic sphere.

"大和なでGUCCI" は銀座で買い物をすると同時に、色々な政治活動に参加しようとしているかもしれません。

Yamato nadeGucci may indeed shop at the Ginza but who is to say that she does not also have an eye on stirring debate in the Japanese Diet.

今の日本の女性は、自由を楽しまないと後悔すると
信じています。

MON

TUE

WED

SAT

SUN

Today's Japanese woman believes that she will be
a fool not to explore her freedom to the full.

"大和なでGUCCI"はすべてのものごとにせっきょくてきに参加します。なぜならば女性達の教育レベルが高くなったからです。これは進んだ国の特徴ですから大変良い事
です。

Yamato nadeGucci has her hand in every pie. And why not? With her advanced education and her natural charm she can hold her own in any setting, public or private. Now, isn't this advancement of women one of the characteristics of a progressive nation?

"大和なでGUCCI" はダイアモンドのようにどこか
らでもかがやきます。

Yamato nadeGucci is like a brilliant diamond
scintillating at every turn.

このことは女性本来の伝統的な"大和なでしこ"の
精神が現代の"大和なでGUCCI"の中にあることを
表しています。

She seems like a new phenomenon but it may
be that she is not much different from the wise,
supportive Japanese woman of old, and that within
the Yamato nadeshiko of the Japanese man's dream
there was always a Yamato nadeGucci just waiting
for the right time to pop out. That day has come!!!

The Changing Japanese Woman:

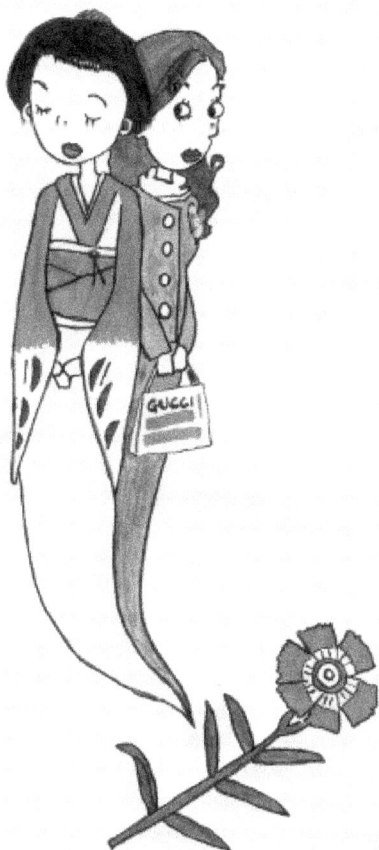

From Yamatonadeshiko to YamatonadeGucci

About the author

Everett Ofori is a Canadian writer. He holds an MBA from Heriot-Watt University and is currently pursuing a Doctorate in Business Administration (DBA) degree with Southern Cross University, NSW, Australia.

About the illustrator

Ahn Soo Kyoung is an artist from South Korea.